Write That Book

Tips For New Authors

by
Michelle G Cameron

Write That Book

Published by:
Michelle G Cameron LLC

ISBN print: 978-0-692-15731-2

Library of Congress Control Number: pending
Categories: Non-Fiction
Printed in the United States of America

Review

Michelle Cameron has done more than write a book about authorship; she has done us a favor. Whether you are an aspiring author, or a seasoned professional, there are tips and great insight in this book that will open your eyes to the joy of authorship. I wish that I had had Write That Book in my life five years ago when I was sitting down to write my first book. It would have made a world of difference for me.

Michelle does an incredible job of giving very practical information in an easily digestible format. In Write That Book, she speaks to everything from how to get started, to how to locate a quality editor, and everything in between. It is one thing to learn from bumping your head a few times, and another thing to learn from an expert. Michelle has presented an expertly written manual for the driven author, and the procrastinating would be author. She has alleviated all of the excuses, and has given us exactly what we need to start and thrive as authors. Praise to Michelle G. Cameron for a well-written manual for authors.

David A. Burrus, Bestselling Author, Business & Relationship Coach

Dedication

This book is dedicated to every person who has struggled with the concept of writing a book. You know that you have a message to share with the world, but you aren't sure how to go about it. It is my desire to help as many people as possible to write all the books that they have inside their hearts. You have a story to tell that will help someone else!

It is my hope that this book will be the start of an amazing journey for you.

Table of Contents

Introduction

Several years ago, I was where you are right now. I knew I had a story to share with the world, but I had no idea how to go about it. First, I wondered if anyone would even want to read my story. Second, I wondered if it was prohibitively expensive to get it out there, and third, I wondered if I had the guts to publish it.

I'm sure by now you've realized that I faced all these obstacles and, one by one, I overcame them. To date, I have successfully published three books, with more on the way! This book is intended to show you in simple steps how to get from where you are right now to where I am.

For starters, there is more than one way to publish a book. Take a deep breath and allow that to soak in. I will mention them as well and share in detail what methods worked for me.

So, let's get started, because I want you to feel confident and ready to tell us your story.

Let's Write That Book!

The Basics of Writing a Book

Writing a book is not as difficult as you think. The hardest part is making the decision to write. Once you have crossed over that mental hurdle, the rest falls into place quite easily.

So, How Do I Start?

First, determine the topic you would like to explore in your book. Keep in mind that you want to write about a topic that you are passionate about. Your excitement and enthusiasm will shine through the pages and will make your reader want to finish your book and recommend it to others.

What's Next?

Next, think of a title that expresses the content of the book. Is the title appealing? Will someone want to grab it off the shelf if they see it in a bookstore? Here's a tip: Search for your title online at Amazon or another book retailer. If it's unique, consider keeping that title.

Now decide what your book sections will be about. Build your Table of Contents around that. Some people write better without a Table of Contents first; they add it after writing the book. Whichever works for you, go with it.

Next, you will want to think of a way to introduce your book – the Introduction. Keep your introduction short and lively so your reader will want to keep reading.

Many authors seek the endorsement of someone who is either a respected expert on the topic they are writing about, or they will approach someone who knows them well and who understands why they chose to write on that topic. This person's endorsement is usually written and printed as the Foreword. This is typically found in the front of the book. This is not a required section for a printed book, but it helps readers understand the context in which the book was written. There is also an optional section named an Afterword, with the same purpose as a Foreword. The Afterword is placed at the back of the book.

You may also decide to dedicate your book to individuals who mean a lot to you. This is also an optional section for printed books.

Writing The Body Of The Book

Here is the part that many new authors (and seasoned ones too!) struggle with – the actual book! If you prefer, use a five-subject notebook to give you a feel of how you want to "say it." You may decide to write or type a certain number of words or pages per day, or per week. Whatever you decide to do, keep a regular schedule so that you stay on-task. I've met several people with unfinished books, simply because they did not set time aside to write.

• • •

Writing Tips

1. Not everything you write will end up in print. Writing is definitely an art, and saying what is on your heart may not look as flowery as the book you may have bought recently. Take comfort in knowing that books start as rough drafts, so the final product will be more polished than at the start.

2. You don't have to write your book in the order of the Table of Contents (TOC). The TOC serves as a guide so that you have a basis or foundation for your thoughts on that topic. If you feel like writing the conclusion on the first day and the second chapter on the second day, go ahead. Remember that the order can be changed later.

3. Do not try to edit or modify anything while you write. JUST. WRITE.

4. All the chapters or topics may not take up the same amount of space, so do not get concerned too much with chapter lengths. (Note: Try to stay away from excessively lengthy chapters.)

5. If you are really struggling to write and need some guidance, contact me for coaching help. For details on my literary coaching service, visit
https://bit.ly/authorconsults

6. Also, you may be able to get a friend to keep you accountable. My first book was written that way. I had to write 10 pages weekly or I owed them money. Believe me, it worked!

7. For some individuals, audio recordings are a great way to start a book. Record, and then type the information as soon as possible.

8. Come up with a deadline for completing your manuscript. You want to be able to say that you did it!

Add Your Notes

_____

_____

_____

_____

_____

_____

_____

_____

_____

_____

_____

_____

_____

_____

_____

_____

_____

_____

_____

_____

_____

Add Your Notes

_____

_____

_____

_____

_____

_____

_____

_____

_____

_____

_____

_____

_____

_____

_____

_____

_____

_____

_____

_____

_____

_____

_____

Editing Tips for New Authors

Every book and author is unique; therefore no two books are ever alike. What readers are expecting to see, however, is excellent work when they pick up your book. As an experienced editor and a technical writer by trade, I have seen quite a bit, and I want to share some important tips to help you as you write.

1. Choose titles that match the contents of your book.

For example, if you are writing about marriage, ensure that most, or 100% of the content addresses married couples.

2. If you take information from a source, mention the source.

Plagiarism is a serious offense and it can cause issues if it's unaddressed before your book is published. Ensure that every quote is referenced, and include book titles, page numbers and authors. You may have noticed them in other books; there's either a Reference page, a Bibliography, footnotes or some other reference style.

3. Be mindful of very long chapters or excessively lengthy manuscripts.

Serious readers can get through thick trilogies and series with ease. With time limits and other life distractions, most readers are looking for books with fewer pages. Stay as much as possible within or around the 100-page target. Unless your book is exciting or enticing, your book will not be read from cover to cover. Keep your chapters short, and to-the-point as possible so that readers can feel that they're making progress as they read your book. One suggestion to help new writers to visualize this is to pick up a popular book and flip through it. Pay attention to the length of the book and the length of each chapter.

4. Write with a dictionary and thesaurus handy.

It helps to ensure that the word(s) you are using are being used as intended. Be aware of the differences between common words such as, "know" vs. "no;" also "they're," "their," and "there;" "won't" vs. "want;" and so on. They may sound the same, but they aren't interchangeable.

5. Take a look at writings to get a good feel for punctuation norms.

For example, ensure that you aren't confusing readers by placing question marks when it isn't a question, or vice versa.

6. Try reading your writing out loud to see if it flows.

If you aren't sure if something sounds right, try reading your manuscript out loud.

7. Consider having a friend proofread your manuscript.

If you have doubts about the content or your writing style, consider sharing your manuscript with a trusted friend for constructive feedback.

8. Collect great reviews for your book content so you can print them in your book.

Approach people who you respect that can speak to your work, and request reviews of your content. If you need to draft a confidentiality agreement before they review, feel free to do so.

Add Your Notes

Add Your Notes

_____

_____

_____

_____

_____

_____

_____

_____

_____

_____

_____

_____

_____

_____

_____

_____

_____

_____

_____

_____

_____

_____

Who Will I Need?

An Editor

An author whom I met recently said to me, "An editor can make or break a book." This is a very true statement. Some authors write and decide to skip the editorial step, and then they wonder why their book is not doing well after launch. Editing brings out the heart of your story and helps with flow, grammar and even the order of sections or events in your book. Great editors will offer alternate ways to say something, or will question the content if it sounds unbelievable, or unrealistic. They see the content through the eyes of your readers, and they want your message to shine through.

A Graphic Designer

A graphic designer partners with you to produce an outstanding product on the bookshelf. Sometimes we can design something for our own personal use via software, but the skill of a graphic designer goes beyond a simple design. They will use your title and book synopsis (and any preferred graphics or photos) to produce an eye-catching cover that will draw attention to your book and help with book sales. People will want to pass your book along when it has an amazing cover.

Note that you may discover a need for other items to help you promote your book or build your brand, such as business cards. Consider getting references from respected associates and friends who have used graphic design services recently.

A Publisher

There are many publishers now, and pricing is as varied as the services they provide and the level of professionalism they offer. Publishing the book is the most expensive aspect of the writing process, but with the right publisher the costs can be minimal without sacrificing quality. Many authors have opted to publish the book themselves, which requires a lot of patience and attention to detail – and time. CreateSpace on Amazon is very popular among many who choose this route. Because I have a full schedule and I like the expert touch of a seasoned publisher, I prefer using them versus doing everything myself. Actually, to clarify, small-scale publishers are considered a form of self-publishing, except they do all the leg-work for you to produce your book. Ensure that you are getting all the components needed for a successful book launch. Ask about registering your book with Library of Congress, assigning an ISBN number, select pricing and other important items. Traditional publishers are the household names such as Thomas Nelson, HarperCollins, and so on.

A Website Designer

One thing that may be needed to help you along the way is an eye-catching website to direct others to learn more about you and your book. This is a significant investment, so you want to go with someone who will give you what you need. You will want a user-friendly website that you can modify/maintain without always needing to hire someone. Consider requesting references from individuals who have websites that you admire.

Ghostwriting

Ghostwriting is a service that is offered to individuals who may not have the time to sit and write their own story. A great ghostwriter will take your concepts for each topic in your book and write you a masterpiece that reflects your thoughts on that topic. An excellent ghostwriter will ensure that the book reflects your voice; that it sounds like you wrote it. Ghostwriting is a confidential agreement between the writer and the actual author, the owner of the content. The book is published in the author's name, and not in the writer's name, hence the term "ghostwriter." Note that ghostwriting can be very expensive, depending on various factors such as the number of pages desired for the book, for example. Reiterations, multiple edits/changes and rush orders may push the price even higher. This option works very well for high-profile individuals.

Note: To have a great ghostwriting experience, ensure that you have clear notes and an outline that they can use to generate your book. Include the target audience and how do you see your book being used (In book clubs? As a workbook? etc.).

Add Your Notes

Add Your Notes

The Book Launch: Telling The World About It

After you've written, edited and published your book, you need to celebrate! After all, you have agonized over it and worked hard to create it! Have a launch party!

Inviting your best supporters is highly recommended, as you desire book sales at your event. Ideally, you will want to leave the event with very few or no books. If your book topic has a broad appeal, consider reaching out to various outlets to market your event. Flyers, business cards, interviews, radio, television and newspaper announcements help to spread the word on your book before the event. If your venue can accommodate a large crowd, then this would be ideal. Also consider your ability to print enough copies to satisfy the attendees, keeping in mind that there is a minimal wholesale cost per book.

Add Your Notes

Add Your Notes

_____

_____

_____

_____

_____

_____

_____

_____

_____

_____

_____

_____

_____

_____

_____

_____

_____

_____

_____

_____

_____

_____

After The Book Launch: What's Next?

You have written the book and hosted your launch event. What do you do now? Be aware that marketing your book will be a significant investment, which may continue several years after you've written your book. The overall success of your book is your responsibility.

Marketing

Marketing your book covers many areas: video, television, radio interviews, advertisements, events, social media, ventures, etc. It will be important to understand the market for your book's content, and offer your book to the right audience. Hiring a marketing firm or independent public relations person, with a proven track record is your ideal scenario. They will be able to secure opportunities for you to get your book before the right people. If you are not able to hire someone to market your book, here are a few tips that can put your information out there.

Blogging – Consider starting a new blog. It can be a written blog or a v-log. Ensure that the content is related to the theme of your book.

Contributing Writer – Search for writing opportunities on visible blogs or online magazines to expand your reach. Many of these are unpaid opportunities, but you may gain new customers that you would not have had access to before.

Vending – If local events are requesting vendors, consider the opportunity to share your book there.

Speaking Invitations – As a speaker or panelist at an event, you should be able to sell copies of your books there. Confirm with the event host.

Book Clubs – Offer your book as a suggestion for book clubs.

Author Conferences – There are quite a few events that target authors specifically. Look for those events in your area and get involved.

These are just a few of the ways to get your book into the hands of your targeted customer base.

Add Your Notes

Add Your Notes

Conclusion

This book was designed to be a quick reference guide for you to pursue your dream of becoming an author. I hope that this short book was a huge help!

Parting Thought
You are not too young or too old to write that book.
Get started today!

Acknowledgments

I would like to acknowledge my family, close friends and associates who have supported me with my previous books and celebrated every milestone with me up to this point.

Special thanks to David A. Burrus, who inspired me to keep writing! Also, thank you to my long-time friend and coach, Linda Grosvenor Holland, a writer extraordinaire herself!

I definitely must give thanks to my Savior, Jesus Christ. I believe in His grace, His forgiveness, His love and His mercy. I am always encouraged and inspired when I reflect on His words in the Bible. I desire, more than anything, to live out what I believe with passion and fervor.

Contact Me!

Facebook: https://www.facebook.com/MGCameronWritingCoach

Twitter: https://twitter.com/MGCameronLLC

Instagram: https://instagram.com/michellegcameronllc

Email: info@michellegcameron.com

LinkedIn: http://bit.ly/MichelleLinkedIn

Website: https://www.michellegcameron.com